5/05

Pebble™ Plus

Bugs, Bugs, Bugs!

Ants

by Margaret Hall

Consulting Editor: Gail Saunders-Smith, PhD

Consultant: Gary A. Dunn, MS, Director of Education
Young Entomologists' Society Inc.
Lansing, Michigan

Capstone *press*

Mankato, Minnesota

Pebble Plus is published by Capstone Press
151 Good Counsel Drive, P.O. Box 669, Mankato, Minnesota 56002
www.capstonepress.com

1 2 3 4 5 6 09 08 07 06 05 04

Library of Congress Cataloging-in-Publication Data
Hall, Margaret, 1947–
    Ants/by Margaret Hall.
    p. cm.—(Pebble plus: Bugs, bugs, bugs!)
    Includes bibliographical references and index.
    ISBN 0-7368-2586-X (hardcover)
    1. Ants—Juvenile literature. [1. Ants.] I. Title. II. Series.
QL568.F7H19 2005
595.79′6—dc22   2003024962

Summary: Simple text and photographs describe the physical characteristics and habits of ants.

Editorial Credits
Sarah L. Schuette, editor; Linda Clavel, series designer; Kelly Garvin, photo researcher; Karen Hieb,
    product planning editor

Photo Credits
Bill Johnson, 8–9
Bruce Coleman Inc./Dale R. Thompson, 5; John Shaw, 17; Raymond Tercafs, 15
Digital Vision, 1
Dwight R. Kuhn, 12–13
Minden Pictures/Mark Moffett, 11, 18–19
Pete Carmichael, cover, 7, 20–21

Note to Parents and Teachers

The Bugs, Bugs, Bugs! series supports national science standards related to the diversity
of life and heredity. This book describes and illustrates ants. The images support early
readers in understanding the text. The repetition of words and phrases helps early
readers learn new words. This book also introduces early readers to subject-specific
vocabulary words, which are defined in the Glossary section. Early readers may need
assistance to read some words and to use the Table of Contents, Glossary, Read More,
Internet Sites, and Index/Word List sections of the book.

Word Count: 96
Early-Intervention Level: 11

Table of Contents

Ants

What are ants?

Ants are insects.

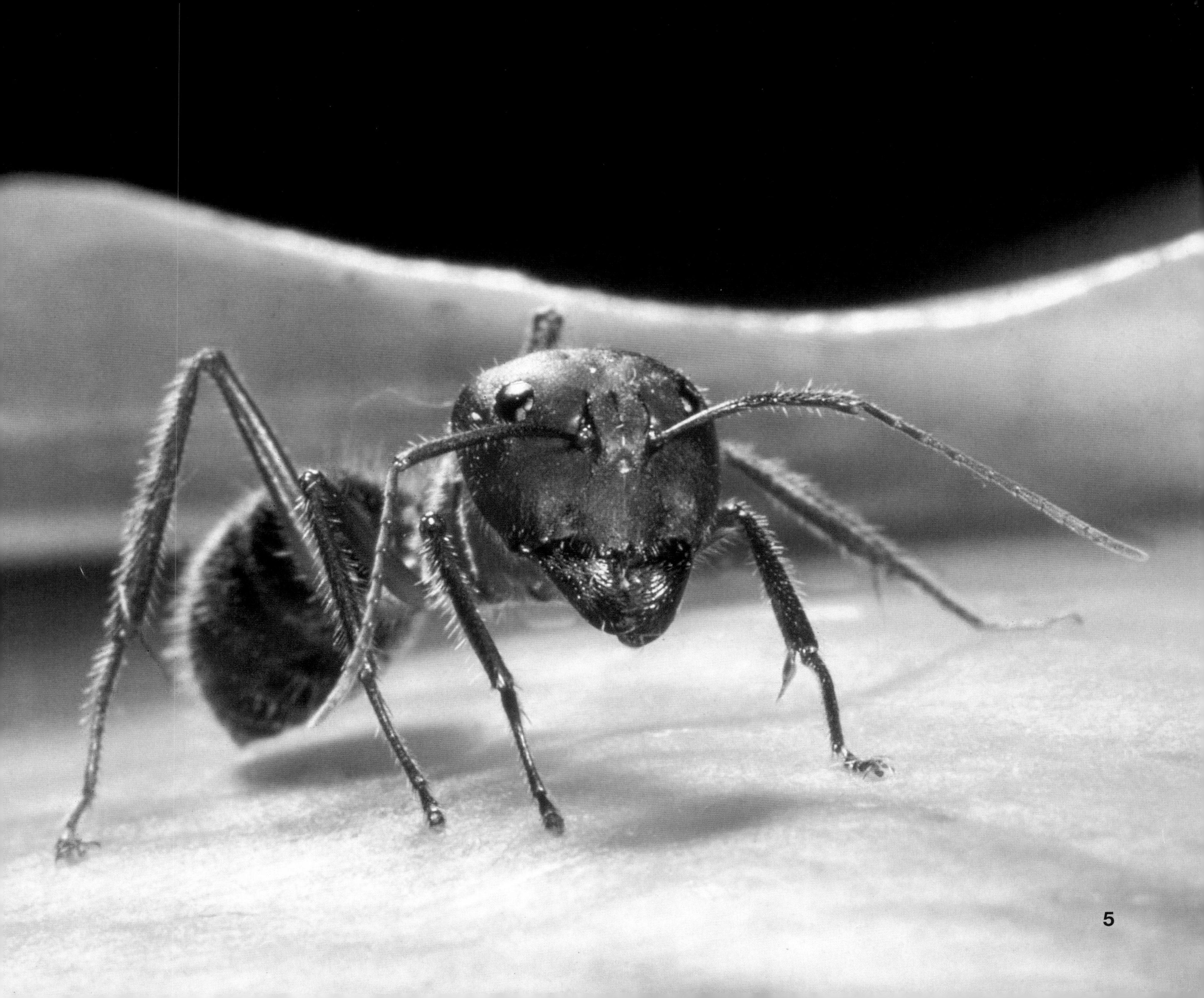

How Ants Look

Ants are about the size
of a sunflower seed.
Ants have six legs.

7

Most ants have black
or brown bodies. Ants
also can be other colors.

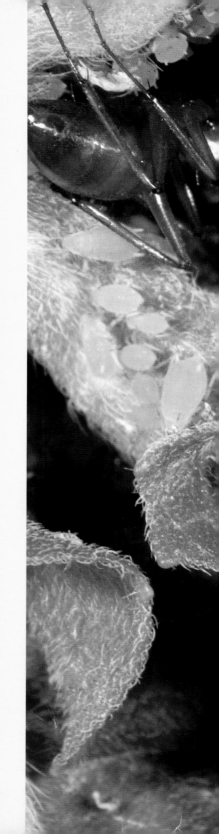

Ants have sharp jaws. Ants chomp and chew with their jaws.

11

Ants have two antennas.

They touch, smell, and

listen with their antennas.

13

What Ants Do

Ants live together in
big colonies.

Ants work together.

Some ants build nests
under the ground.

Queen ants lay eggs.
Worker ants take care
of eggs.

worker ant

Worker ants find food.
They carry leaves, fruit,
and other insects back
to the nest.

Glossary

antenna—a feeler; insects use antennas to sense movement, to smell, and to listen to each other.

colony—a large group of ants that live together; some ant colonies can have millions of ants.

insect—a small animal with a hard outer shell, six legs, three body sections, and two antennas; most insects have wings.

jaw—a part of the mouth used to grab, bite, and chew

queen ant—an adult female ant that lays eggs; most colonies have only one queen ant.

worker ant—an adult female ant that does not lay eggs; worker ants build nests, find food, and take care of young ants.

Read More

Barner, Bob. *Bug Safari*. New York: Holiday House, 2004.

Nelson, Kristin L. *Busy Ants*. Pull Ahead Books. Minneapolis: Lerner, 2004.

Tagliaferro, Linda. *Ants and Their Nests*. Animal Homes. Mankato, Minn.: Capstone Press, Pebble Plus, 2004.

Internet Sites

FactHound offers a safe, fun way to find Internet sites related to this book. All of the sites on FactHound have been researched by our staff.

Here's how:

1. Visit *www.facthound.com*

2. Type in this special code **073682586X** for age-appropriate sites. Or enter a search word related to this book for a more general search.

3. Click on the **Fetch It** button.

FactHound will fetch the best sites for you!

Index/Word List